WOMAN

-- FEB 2019

Charlotte Coleman-Smith

CONTENTS

Collins

Unladylike behaviour?

Women first began to fly planes at the beginning of the 20th century. In those days, they were expected to be mothers, wives and **obedient** daughters – not pilots!

Many people thought women didn't have the strength to fly a plane, or weren't clever enough. Flying was seen as unladylike. It was also very dangerous. Early female aviators, or pilots, had to be **stubborn**, confident and very brave.

Log book

"Aviation (flying planes) is for grown men – **alert**, strong, sturdy and, above all, capable of **endurance**. Such qualities are not often found in women."

French pilot,
André Beaumont, 1912

First flights

In 1903, a 19-year-old Cuban-American, Aida de Acosta, became the first woman to fly a powered aircraft **solo**. She had three lessons from Alberto Santos-Dumont, a Brazilian – all of them on the ground! She then climbed into the basket of his airship and flew a short distance. Alberto followed her on his bicycle, shouting instructions!

Aida de Acosta

In 1908, Frenchwoman Thérèse Peltier flew across the Military Square in Turin, Italy. This is thought to be the first flight by a woman in a plane heavier than air.

Thérèse Peltier

The Wright brothers' sister

The first powered plane ever to fly was built by American brothers, Orville and Wilbur Wright. On 17 December 1903, Orville Wright took off from a sand dune at Kitty Hawk in North Carolina, USA, and flew his plane for 12 seconds.

The Wright brothers are very famous but they also had a sister, Katharine, who was an important part of their success. Katharine went with them on tours and even flew in the plane with them. This made her one of the first women in the air.

Orville, Katharine and Wilbur Wright

Log book

"If ever the world thinks of us in connection with aviation, it must remember our sister."

Wilbur Wright

Early flying machines

The first planes were built of light materials like wood and canvas. They were biplanes, meaning that they had two wings stacked one above the other. The first airmail flights – carrying letters and light objects – were made using biplanes.

a biplane flying in 1910

As planes flew faster, higher and for longer distances, metal parts and panels were used, until planes were eventually made entirely of metal.

How do they stay in the air? The wings of a plane are shaped so that air flows faster over the top than the bottom. This builds up pressure underneath the wings, which pushes the plane upwards, against **gravity**.

a Boeing P-26, *Glendale*

THE FIRST LADIES OF THE AIR

After Aida de Acosta and Katharine Wright, there came many more female aviators. These women went on ever-longer journeys, breaking records and risking their lives to discover more about flight.

Flying was an expensive hobby, so female pilots were often from rich families. Mrs Spencer Cleaver, daughter of the Minister of Finance of Northern Ireland, was a keen aviator who flew from England to India in 1929 with her **co-pilot**, Captain Drew. She had extra fuel tanks fitted to her plane so that she could breakfast in London, shop in Paris and return in time for dinner in London!

Mrs Spencer Cleaver

On 29 August 1911, Hilda Hewlett became the first British woman to pass her pilot's test. She set up a flying school at the Brooklands motor-racing circuit in Surrey, UK.

Less than a year later, on 16 April 1912, American journalist, Harriet Quimby, became the first woman to cross the English Channel. She wore a purple flying outfit and was quite a celebrity. She was killed in a flying accident in 1937.

In the early days of flight, the **cockpit** was open. Female pilots and passengers had to tie their skirts round their ankles. Later, they would wear more practical, all-in-one outfits; leather coats, and goggles to protect their eyes against the wind.

Women pilots began to wear more practical clothing.

Spectacular stunts

Crowds flocked to watch daring female pilots perform **death-defying** stunts – women such as American, Katherine Stinson. In 1915, she was the first ever woman to do a **vertical** loop – and in a plane she'd built herself!

Phoebe Fairgrave Omlie performed stunts on moving planes in the 1920s and 1930s. She danced the **Charleston** on the top wing and hung from the plane by her teeth!

Florence "Pancho" Barnes was born into a rich Californian family but was determined not to live the quiet life of a lady. She started training horses, competing in air races and flying stunt planes for Hollywood films. She became a respected pilot, and the holder of a world speed record.

Pancho opened a hotel in the desert, called the Happy Bottom Riding Club. This was very popular with pilots and movie stars. Her incredible story has been told in films and books.

Florence "Pancho" Barnes

9

WOMEN AT WAR

World War One (1914–1918) was the first time planes had been used in battles. We usually think of pilots in World War One as men, but some women did become pilots of bomber planes.

Frenchwoman, Marie Marvingt, was so annoyed at not being allowed to fight that she disguised herself as a man and joined the soldiers in the **trenches**. In 1915, she was the first woman in the world to fly bombing missions. She was given a special medal for her bravery.

Marie was also a brilliant athlete and a nurse. She worked hard to try and set up an air ambulance service to help injured people get to hospital more quickly.

Mademoiselle Marie MARVINGT prend le départ au Centre d'aviation de Bétheny *1914*

Hélène Dutrieu – a Belgian cycling champion known as "The Human Arrow" for her love of speed – made flights from Paris to check on the movement of German troops.

Breaking down barriers

It was difficult enough for those women who had money and came from "respectable" families to learn to fly. In the days when black people in America were seen to be **inferior** to whites, Bessie Coleman had an even harder battle.

As a black woman, Bessie wasn't allowed to take lessons in America, so she saved up money working as a **manicurist** in a barber's shop, learnt French and travelled to Paris to learn to fly. Bessie was the first African-American woman to earn a pilot's licence.

Bessie Coleman's pilot's licence

Bessie got her licence on 15 June 1921; then began performing stunts and demonstrations at airshows. Her great wish was to make flying possible for women and men equally, and for people of any skin colour. She died in a plane crash in 1926 at the age of 34.

Log book

"No one had heard of a black woman pilot in 1919. I refused to take no for an answer."

Bessie Coleman

THE WOMEN'S AIR DERBY

The 1920s and 1930s were exciting years for pilots.
After World War One, planes were faster and more **reliable**,
and flying was now possible for more and more people.

On 18 August 1929, a pistol shot gave the signal for
19 women to fly 4,440 kilometres from Santa Monica,
California, to Cleveland,
Ohio, in a race called
the Women's Air Derby.

USA

Cleveland

Santa Monica

getting the planes
ready, Santa Monica

Most of the cockpits were open, and the planes were lightweight and very basic. The pilots had no **radars** or **air-traffic controllers** to tell them where to go.

This dangerous race was important for female aviators – it proved to the world that they could fly as well as, if not better than, men.

Over nine days, two planes crashed, others ran out of fuel, and one pilot was killed. But 15 women did finish. A huge crowd gathered at the finish line in Cleveland to welcome Louise Thaden, who came first.

Louise Thaden

LONG-DISTANCE FLIGHTS

As well as breaking speed records, female aviators began trying new routes that took them across the Atlantic Ocean, to South Africa and to Australia, and across the North and South Poles.

5

8

7

1 Lady Mary Heath, 1928
Cape Town to Goodwood

2 Mary Russell, 1929
Kent to Karachi

3 Mary Russell, 1930
Kent to Cape Town

4 Amy Johnson, 1930
Croydon to Darwin

Amelia Earhart, 1932
Across the Atlantic
Ocean (west to east)

6 Jean Batten, 1934
Kent to Darwin

7 Amelia Earhart, 1935
Honolulu to California

8 Beryl Markham, 1936
Across the Atlantic
Ocean (east to west)

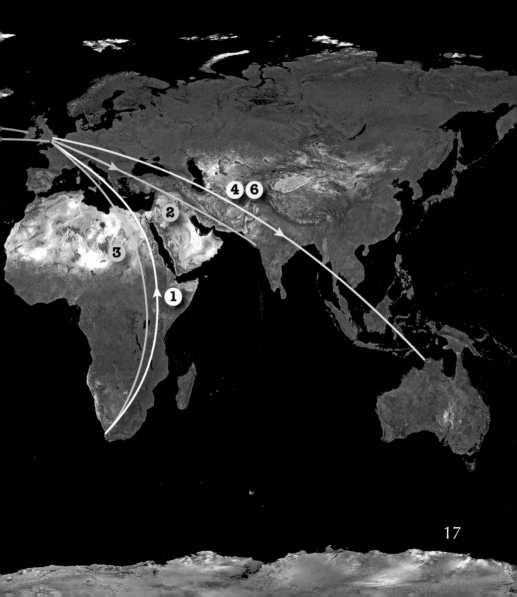

The biggest challenge faced by the earliest pilots was **navigation**. After World War One, pilots were starting to use radio, but this was very basic. Imagine being in a plane in the dark, or in poor weather, without lights, a mobile phone or satnav!

Before setting off, pilots **plotted** the course, checked the weather forecast and worked out how long it should take to fly a certain distance at a certain speed. This was called "dead reckoning".

Planes flew low, and the pilot would look out of the window to find landmarks – cities, rivers, towers – which they could compare with their map. Sometimes, bonfires, or **beacons**, were lit along the way.

If the cockpit was open, freezing temperatures and high winds made air navigation very uncomfortable. Heavy gloves and cold fingers didn't make it any easier!

Celestial navigation (using the stars and sun) was another important way early aviators could find out where they were. Of course, even bad weather, or a simple cloud, made this difficult.

In the late 1920s, a US Navy officer named Philip Van Horn Weems set up schools to teach pilots about celestial navigation. This was called "The Weems System". Weems also showed pilots how to set their watches by listening to radio broadcasts, and how to use **Morse code**.

Pilots used instruments like this sextant to help them navigate by using the stars and the sun.

Amy Johnson

Two successful long-distance pilots were Amy Johnson from Britain and Amelia Earhart from the USA.

On 5 May 1930, Amy took off from Croydon, UK, in her Gypsy Moth plane, "Jason". 18,000 kilometres later, she landed in Darwin, Australia. The journey took her 19 days and she became the first female to fly solo from England to Australia. Over the next five years, Amy broke records flying to Moscow, Cape Town and India.

On 5 January 1941, her plane crashed into the Thames Estuary, miles from where it should have been. Some claim she was shot down. Others say she was on a secret mission. Her body was never found.

Log book

"You relax ... your head drops ... you sit up with a jerk. Where are you? Oh yes ... in the middle of the North Atlantic with hungry waves below you like **vultures** ..."

Amy Johnson

Amelia Earhart

In 1932, Amelia Earhart became the first woman to fly across the Atlantic Ocean, from west to east, and to fly solo across the Pacific (Honolulu to California), in 1935.

On 20 May 1932, Amelia left Newfoundland, at the start of her journey across the Atlantic Ocean. Bad weather forced her to land in a farmer's field in County Derry, Northern Ireland. She told the **astonished** family she had no luggage, and had drunk only tomato juice since leaving.

On 1 June 1937, Amelia and her **navigator**, Fred Noonan, took off from Miami, Florida, USA, in an attempt to fly around the world, following the **equator**. On 2 July, their plane disappeared in the Pacific Ocean, near Howland Island. It's thought they may have run out of fuel. Their plane was never found.

Log book

"Women must try to do things as men have tried. When they fail, their failure must be but a challenge to others."

Amelia Earhart

WORLD WAR TWO

World War Two (1939–1945) saw
many new heroines.
Amongst these was American,
Jacqueline Cochran.
In 1941, Cochran was
the first woman to
fly a bomber across
the Atlantic Ocean.
Later, she was put in charge
of the US Women Airforce
Service Pilots (WASPs). In 1953,

Jacqueline
Cochran

Cochran was also the first woman
to break the sound barrier (to fly faster than the speed of
sound). She holds more speed, distance and **altitude** world
records than any other pilot, male
or female.

In Soviet Russia, many
young women flew
bombing raids at night.
The German nickname
for them was *Nachthexen*
(Night Witches).

SPECIAL DELIVERIES

Women didn't only fly in bombing raids. In the UK, pilots in the Air Transport Auxiliary (ATA) flew planes from factories to military airfields. In the USA, the WASPs delivered bombers to the battlefront.

Log book

"It really was the best job ... because it was exciting, and we could help the war effort. Flying ... was the nearest you could get to having your own wings."

Joy Lofthouse, who flew a Spitfire during World War Two

an ATA pilot

WASP pilots

PASSENGER PLANES

Despite years of death-defying stunts, record-breaking long-distance flights and brave wartime service, it was still a long time before women were allowed to be in charge of **commercial planes**.

On 31 December 1934, Helen Richey became the first woman to fly a commercial airliner in the USA, but wasn't allowed to fly in bad weather!

Yvonne Pope Sintes

Yvonne Pope Sintes started out as an air hostess, but always dreamt of flying a plane herself. In 1972, she became the first female captain of a commercial plane in the UK.

Log book

"When I first started, one of the pilots said he would **resign** if a woman joined ... unfortunately, he didn't."

Yvonne Pope Sintes

the first three female British Airways pilots, 1987

Into space

Women had **conquered** the skies – next stop, space!

On 12 April 1961, Yuri Gagarin became the first man in space. Only two years later, in 1963, another Russian, Valentina Tereshkova, became the first female – proving again that women could do the same as men.

Valentina Tereshkova

Eileen Collins, 23 July 1999
NASA's first woman Space
Shuttle commander

Helen Sharman, 18 May 1991
the first person from Britain to
go into space

Svetlana Savitskaya, 25 July 1984
the first woman to walk in space

Modern heroines

Today, there are women in space, women piloting large jumbo jets and stunt planes, and women fighter pilots.

In 2013, Flight Lieutenant Ayesha Farooq was Pakistan's first female war pilot.

Patty Wagstaff was the first woman to be US National Aerobatic Champion. She flies commercial planes and helicopters, teaches aerobatics, gives displays and performs stunts in movies and television.

In 2013, British pilot, Tracey Curtis-Taylor, flew from South Africa to the UK, following the same route taken in 1928 by Lady Mary Heath. In 2015, she repeated Amy Johnson's 1930 flight from England to Australia.

However, only a very small number of commercial pilots are female (around three to five per cent). Women and girls may not realise that being a pilot is a real job they could have in the future.

For most people, it's still a dream to fly – but for our future female aviators, it's a dream that *can* become a reality.

1920s ...

... today

GLOSSARY

air-traffic controllers	people whose job it is to give instructions to pilots by radio
alert	wide-awake and watchful
altitude	height above Earth
astonished	very surprised
beacons	fires lit as a signal to help pilots see the way
Charleston	a lively dance from the 1920s
cockpit	the space in a plane where the pilot sits
commercial planes	planes with paying passengers on board
conquered	defeated, gained control over
co-pilot	a pilot who can take over from the main pilot of a plane
death-defying	daring and brave, risking death
endurance	having the strength to keep going in a difficult situation
equator	imaginary circle around the earth, halfway between the North and South Poles
gravity	the force that keeps objects on the ground and causes them to fall to Earth when dropped
inferior	of lower quality or value
manicurist	a person who does beauty treatments for the hands and nails
Morse code	a system of sending messages using long and short sounds
NASA	the National Aeronautics and Space Administration (USA), in charge of aviation and space flight

28

navigation	the act of directing a plane (or ship, or car) from one place to another
navigator	a person who finds out which route to take
obedient	willing to obey, to do as you are told
plotted	planned on a map
radars	instruments that send out radio waves to find out exactly where planes are
reliable	able to be trusted
resign	leave a job
solo	on your own
stubborn	determined, strong-willed
trenches	long, narrow ditches dug during World War One, where soldiers sheltered and prepared to fight
vertical	straight up and down; upright
vultures	birds of prey that feed on dead flesh

INDEX

FANTASTIC FLIGHT PATH

1912 Harriet Quimby first woman to fly across the English Channel

1930 Amy Johnson first woman to fly solo from the UK to Australia

1903 Aida de Acosta first solo flight by a woman

1915 Katherine Stinson first woman to perform a vertical loop

1908 Thérèse Peltier first solo flight by a woman in plane heavier than air

1921 Bessie Coleman first African-American woman to earn a pilot's licence

1915 Marie Marvingt first woman to go on a bombing mission

1911 Hilda Hewlett first British woman to pass a pilot's test

1934 Helen Richey first woman to fly a commercial airliner (good weather only!)

1932 Amelia Earhart first woman to fly across the Atlantic Ocean

1935 Amelia Earhart first woman to fly solo across the Pacific Ocean

1972 Yvonne Pope Sintes first female captain of a commercial plane in the UK

1963 Valentina Tereshkova first woman in space

2013 Ayesha Farooq Pakistan's first female war pilot

1953 Jacqueline Cochran first woman to break the sound barrier

1941 Jacqueline Cochran first woman to fly a bomber plane across the Altantic Ocean

Ideas for reading

Written by Clare Dowdall, PhD
Lecturer and Primary Literacy Consultant

Reading objectives:
- retrieve and record information from non-fiction
- read books that are structured in different ways
- draw inferences and justify these with evidence

Spoken language objectives:
- participate in discussions, presentations, performances, role play, improvisations and debates

Curriculum links: History (beyond 1066)

Resources: ICT, paper and pens, world atlas

Build a context for reading

- Ask children if they would like to be a pilot or an astronaut, and what skills are needed to do this. Challenge children to consider if these jobs can be done by men and women.
- Look at the cover and read the blurb. Discuss what having *courage, grit and determination to conquer the skies* means.
- Read through the contents together. Ask children which sections interest them the most and why.

Understand and apply reading strategies

- Read pp2–3 together. Use the glossary to check that children understand the adjectives *obedient* and *stubborn*, and what these words mean in the context of women aviators.
- Read the final paragraph on p3 carefully. Check that children understand what *in a plane heavier than air* means (not an airship).
- Discuss what a log book is. Walk through the book looking for log book extracts, and establish that they are real accounts, written in the first person, giving actual accounts of events.